Exodus to Advent

God's Christmas Plan for you, and for me

Esther C. Baird

Esther C. Baird

Exodus to Advent
God's Christmas plan for you, and for me
© Esther Baird
2018
All Rights Reserved
www.estherbaird.com

ISBN: 9781728620800

Cover design: Andrew Runion

CONTENTS

CONTENTS

Exodus to Advent

Esther C. Baird

INTRODUCTION

Christmas.

Just typing that word shoots my anxiety through the roof. Here in my 40's, the enchantment and wonder has gotten lost somewhere in the box of homemade salt-dough ornaments I hang every year. They make the branches droop and I secretly wish they'd break already.

I'm known for being an early decorator, an early Christmas music player, and a lover of all things Christmas. But that was because I found November in Boston, with young kids, to be really hard. It gets dark by lunch and always rains, so there was nothing to do but sit around and stare at the gloom. By the weekend after Thanksgiving, I was done with the dreariness and ready for loud festive music, hundreds of twinkle lights, yards of garland, and Dickens Homes. It all snapped me out of the funk.

Then my girls grew older and it turned out November is nothing compared to December. December with school-aged children is chaos, noise and nonsense. It's a whirling dervish of social and school obligations in uncomfortable blouses, and a lot of driving at night (see the aforementioned darkness at lunch point). And on top of all the frenzy, I also had to keep up the Mrs. Claus, tinsel-and-lights, party-planning, I-LOVE-CHRISTMAS spiel.

This last Christmas, as I sat with the women in the Bible study I taught, I confessed, "I'm over Christmas. I'm exhausted and I feel dread, not joy. I feel chaos, not peace." Then there was no time to talk about it, because we all had to scatter to the next million events our schools, church and work required of us.

How had frenzy become the main focus of Christmas? How had we gotten here?

One of the things that gives me great joy is a good Star Wars movie. I even enjoy a bad Star Wars movie. I love knowing that the movie I am watching is part of a larger story that I have loved since I was eight years old. When the latest movies came out and we glimpsed the Millennium Falcon for the first time in decades, I couldn't help but cheer. I knew that space ship so well I could fly it myself! It was in a new Star Wars adventure, but it was clearly part of the larger story that I knew and loved.

Christmas is not just a standalone story about a baby and a manger and some angels. It's a great story that's part of a giant story--part of THE story. And while the baby is the main character in the Christmas story, the same baby is also the main character way back in Exodus.

Remember Exodus? Most people, whether they grew up in the church or not, know about the Israelites and Pharaoh--the plagues and the wandering in the desert. But do they know it's part of the big story? Do you? Or do you read Exodus like a one-off Star Wars movie, not realizing there is an entire canon of films that reveal the story in a way that is more fantastic and amazing than you imagined.

So this Christmas, I may freak out in the school parking lot during class party season, and I may feel a little tense when I put up my Christmas tree and stare down that salt-dough. But I invite you to join me in considering the big story--Exodus to Advent--the Christmas story found in the promises God made His people thousands of years ago, in dusty, old Egypt.

We'll look at baby Moses, the plagues and the Ten Commandments. We'll dig into the tabernacle and God's laws and see how the big story has always been the Christmas story. And it's always been a story about the promises God made to His people then, that are still true today. They are true for you, and they are true for me.

Esther C. Baird

DAY 1: STUCK

It's December, and choices hang over our heads like icicles of impending doom. Do you set out LED lawn lights that create a giant flying snowflake across your house? Or do you put up the inflatable reindeer that is bigger than your car? That's a tough choice. And, if no one else has told you, the answer should be an emphatic *neither*. But even without that disaster of a choice, there is a lot about the holidays that makes us feel swamped. Sometimes we feel a deeper stress because we honestly have no idea what to do next. Decisions and uncertainty can inundate us with fear or anger or old memories or just plain confusion.

Well good news! Christmas is all about God providing a way for those who are stuck, confused, and scraping the bottom of their barrel for answers.

Take for example the beginning of our Christmas story. A young pregnant mom, living an ordinary and impoverished existence. A death threat issued for her child shortly after his birth. There were no options. There was no 911 to call. Nothing she could Google. Just the sure thought that having survived childbirth, her child was now hunted down as a threat to the powers that be.

Mary the mother of Jesus? Sure, of course; you know about her. But do you know about Jochebed? Jochebed, the mother of Moses (not a big hit on a list of popular girl's names, but her name nevertheless).

Both Mary and Jochebed lived in perilous times. Both lived under a ruler who felt threatened by the birth of male babies and ordered them killed to prevent an uprising. And both mothers lived in socially hard contexts--Mary was pregnant before marriage, and Jochebed was forced to hide Moses for three months against the law of Pharaoh himself.

They both must have wondered how it was all going to end. Would their lives ever be the same? And if not, what would the future hold? They both carried babies who would change the world. Who would literally change history as we know it. But first they had to be born, and then survive their early childhoods. How would it all work out?

God knew how. He didn't need to cheat and read the last page of the book first. He wrote both the beginning and the end. He had a giant plan for His people across all of time, and a few narcissistic rulers weren't going to thwart it.

Exodus 2:1-10 states that God gave Jochebed the faith to hide Moses in the little baby ark. That's right, that reed basket Moses so famously floated down the Nile in actually is the same Hebrew word used for the giant big "ark" that Noah built. Water was dangerous and often meant death during ancient times. Floods and river crossings and unpredictable storms at sea posed a constant risk. But water didn't mean death if you were in God's ark. And like Noah holding steady in the flood, baby Moses remained safe in the reeds of the Nile until Pharaoh's daughter found him. God rescued Moses so that Moses could in turn help rescue God's people out of slavery and lead them towards a new country just for them.

And someday, another baby would be born in equally dangerous times.

Mary accepted God's grace through faith to first carry, and then raise, her son. But this baby didn't need to float in an ark, because this baby would grow up to be a human ark. This baby would grow up to say to those who followed Him, "You will know that you are in me, and I am in you." (John 14:20) Jesus keeps us safe as the water and waves crash about us. He shelters us from the storms of life. He is our ark.

I get it. You may not be a pregnant woman living under a hostile regime trying to hunt you down. You may not be weaving baby ark baskets out of reeds or fluffing the hay for your impending manger crib. But you may be stuck.

This advent season when Christmas cheer is crowded out by obligations, self-doubt and concerns, when you're barely treading water as the floods rise and the torrents of life rush you toward an uncertain end, know that God has a perfect destination already created for you, a promised land that He created and invites you to enter.

Just as Moses was born to lead the people out of Egypt into the promised land, Jesus was born to lead us out of this broken land and into an eternal one that can never be harmed. If you follow that second baby, the flood cannot harm you because Jesus is the one carrying you there.

It was true then, and it's true now. For you, and for me.

Esther C. Baird

DAY 2: NORMAL

One of the hardest things at Christmas time is the frenzied pace--cramming more in, rushing from event to event, dashing out to buy a last roll of wrapping paper, hurrying to complete our shopping for the seemingly endless parties. We have nightmares about buying one more stocking stuffer. It's exhausting. Each year my friend and I promise each other, "Never again. Next year we will fix this!" I don't need to tell you--we never do. It's the whole frog in the pot problem, except in my case, it's the mom in December problem. Crazy at Christmas is just normal to me now.

This just goes to show that the human heart is pretty good at making anything seem "normal." Take, for example, the Israelites in Egypt. They were enslaved for 400 years. When they first moved to Egypt under Joseph, they were a special and highly regarded people sojourning as guests during a famine. But with new Pharaohs, their status eroded over time, and they became just another oppressed people group under the greatest power on earth. After 400 years it had just become "normal."

It was so normal that Moses, who was raised in Pharaoh's court, didn't realize his people were mistreated until he grew up. But when he saw an Egyptian beating an

Israelite in Exodus 2:11-15, he reacted and killed the Egyptian to save his fellow countryman's life.

Whether or not it was a defensive killing or a murder is an exciting question you can pose at your next dinner party, but the point is in the Israelites' reaction. Rather than understanding why Moses defended them, they got mad. Mad at the hint of righteous anger Moses showed toward their enslavement. Their oppressed lives were just normal-- no reason to rock Pharaoh's boat.

But God had not called His people to be enslaved. He called them to be *His* people in *His* land with *Him* as their ruler and king. And He was going to use Moses to open their eyes to the promise and the hope of a life free from slavery.

At Christmas we get to celebrate the same promise that we were not born to be enslaved. We can be enslaved to fear of failure, to fear of rejection, to desires for power or money. We can be enslaved to addictions or lifestyles or even to our own children or families. Anything that we allow to control our hearts, other than Jesus, is something we are enslaved to.

The truth is, you may have been acting a certain way for so long now that it just seems normal. So you have a small control issue? It's just normal. So you pursue financial security to the exclusion of your family? How else can you get ahead? So you allow your children to be the main thing you live for? That's great! It's modern parenting. So you wish you just had an easier time keeping your temper? Oh well, a temper is normal.

Nope. No, it's not.

I hate to be a downer, but the honest word for slavery in our context is sin. Our normalized prioritization of anything other than God is the human condition called sin.

But just as Moses was born to free his people, Jesus was born to free His. And we are all invited to be His people. He even says, "Everyone who sins is a slave to sin. Now a

6

slave has no permanent place in the family, but a son belongs to it forever. So if the Son sets you free, you will be free indeed." (John 8:34-36)

He frees us from our slavery. He brings us into His family. Both are forever.

Slavery wasn't supposed to be normal to the Israelites. God was calling them to so much more. And it's not normal for us either. Only following Jesus is normal. This Christmas take a deep breath and consider if you believe God frees you fully. Do you know what true normal feels like? Do you live in God's freedom? Do you believe His freedom is for you? It is.

It was true then, and it's true now. For you, and for me.

Esther C. Baird

DAY 3: KNOWN

My two girls play a card game called *I Doubt It*. It's based on your ability to lie. I don't play card games, so I have no idea what the rules are, I just know that one player states the cards they have and the other players have to guess if they are lying or telling the truth. (Ok as I type that, I realize it sounds a lot like poker. To be determined at another time: are my tween-aged daughters secretly running a gambling ring from our living room?)

At any rate, our eldest daughter never wants me to play or even be in the same room as her when she plays, because that girl couldn't tell a lie to me even if her actual life, instead of a game, depended on it. This past summer they were playing with my mother, and I knew my daughter was lying. As I walked into the kitchen, I heard my my mom ask her if she had a certain card.

"Yes," she replied.

"Please!" I yelled. "She totally does not have it!"

My daughter yelled back, "I do! I'm not lying. I really actually have it."

My mom believed her. Wrong move. My daughter won the round.

She came running in. "How you could you tell? You couldn't even see my face!"

I laughed. I only needed to hear her voice; I just know her.

I realize as she gets older some of my knowing will change. Some day she may be able to beat me at a game of *I Doubt It*. But to be known that well is both scary and freeing. If someone knows you that well, then they know all the bad stuff too. But if that all-knowing person is still hanging around, they must actually like you and want to be with you. And don't we crave that? Don't we want someone to know us so well, the good, the bad and the really messy, and yet still want to be with us?

In Ancient Near East times the gods were not particularly personal. They were to be feared. They certainly weren't sticking around to get to know common, messy, broken regular folks.

But when Moses grew up, he had an encounter with the God of the Israelites that was deeply personal. In Exodus 3 God talked to Moses through the burning bush and told Moses that He saw the suffering of His people. He saw the mess, and He was going to rescue them. Then He told Moses His personal name. Yahweh. It means "I am." It may seem strange that God's personal name is the present tense verb "to be," but there is no past for God and no future. He sees all things, all times; He sees everything you've done and will do. God is all present at all times.

Yet with all that knowledge and power, what God wants is to be with us, and to have us know Him.

God was telling Moses that He would make a way for that inconceivable truth to be a reality. He wanted His people to know His personal name even knowing that the next centuries would be full of idolatry and rejection. God still wanted to rescue them. He still wanted them to be with Him in a land He would make safe for them.

Here on the cusp of Christmas, things are a little strained. Sometimes it's hard for me to be the best friend or wife or mother to those around me. I have to go to a lot of events and make small talk where I'm actually thinking, "If they knew how annoyed I am right now, or how I yelled at my children just before we got here, or how I am making a grocery list during the sermon, they wouldn't actually like me."

But God knows all the deep dark secrets of His people. He knows what we are actually thinking, and He still wants us to know Him! He wants us to know His personal name because He loves us and has a plan to save us. In fact, for us He goes even one step further than revealing His personal name.

He revealed Himself as a person. He sent Jesus. Matthew 1:23 says that Jesus fulfilled the prophecy in Isaiah that He would be born and called Immanuel. Immanuel means "God with us."

Jesus came at Christmas to be God with us. He lived in our world and did all the common, regular, people things. He saw the absolute despair and fear and sin that is in our hearts, and then took all the deepest darkest things and wiped them away by dying for us. Yes, Jesus knows everything you do; and yes, Jesus still wants to be with you. He wants for you to know, really know, Him and His love. Because He really knows and loves you.

You don't have to ever doubt that. It's true. Then, and now. For you, and for me.

Esther C. Baird

DAY 4: HELP

Every year the women's event team at our church produces a Christmas extravaganza in early December. We've done giant yankee swaps, we've done carol sings, we've done garland making, and we've done movies. We always end up making our church's multipurpose room look festive, welcoming and unapologetically ultra-Christmassy. The food is amazing and seasonal, and when there is music, it is near Broadway quality.

It's one of our largest events, and, as the Director of Women's Ministries, I always feel totally panicked because I don't know how to do any of it. I can't decorate a table to save my life. If it were up to me, we'd eat pizza off paper plates and drink wine from paper cups while someone stood up and read Luke 2 with a strand of twinkle lights wrapped around her waist.

Thankfully the women on my team excel at events. One of them can turn $200 into a gourmet Christmas feast for 90 women. Another can take my thematic direction of, "I don't know, something sparkly with Jesus in the middle," and whip up a room that looks like a professional designer came to town. And our musicians bring their voices and instruments so that women can truly celebrate the birth of our Savior through carols and songs.

God put me in this job, but He also gives me the tools and people to accomplish His plans despite my, uh, deficiencies.

So I totally understand Moses' concern when God told him he was going to be the guy to save all of Israel. Even if, as some commentators say, his early demurral reflects cultural humility, he still had to have some anxiety. One guy against the deity king Pharaoh--the greatest power on earth? (Side note: Am I comparing running a women's Christmas event to freeing the Israelites from 400 years of Egyptian rule? You can be the judge... but only if you've run women's events before.)

Thankfully God was doing the rescuing, not Moses. Moses was just going to be the man God used. In Exodus 4:1-17 God upgraded Moses' staff with supernatural miraculous powers and gave him the support and encouragement of his brother Aaron to be with him, to do some public speaking for him, and to stand by Moses as they approached Pharaoh.

God was going to use Moses to save His people. He was going to use him to lead them out of their slavery into the land God had set for them. He was going to use Moses to communicate His very words to Pharaoh and the people. And though He gave Moses the gifts he would need, it was always God doing the work, because at the end of the day, Moses was still a man who needed to be saved too--not just from physical slavery, but from slavery to sin.

At Christmas we get to celebrate that the baby who was born in Bethlehem didn't need any help from God to handle His assignment, because Jesus was God. Like Moses, His assignment was also to free His people from slavery, and lead them into God's promised land, speaking the very words of God directly into our hearts. Unlike Moses, Jesus didn't need to be saved. That's why His life and death are so amazing--He wasn't in any trouble. He came because we were. Jesus puts it simply, "The Son of Man came to look for the lost and save them." (Luke 19:10)

Just as Moses couldn't actually save the people of Israel without God, we can't save ourselves. In spite of all the self-help books, and despite all the Christmas cheer, only Jesus can save us. And He does. He looks for us when we are lost, and He saves us.

For many of us, Christmas can be particularly hard. It may add more things to our already long list of things we don't feel adequate to do. This Christmas remember that God may call us to tasks or situations that feel totally outside our skill set. But if God calls us, He will also provide us with the tools we need to accomplish His plans.

What He calls us to, above all else, is to follow the baby born 2,000 years ago who has already accomplished all that we need in this life and the next. Every single other thing pales in comparison. Do you believe that God can do the saving?

Because it's true. Then, and now. For you, and for me.

DAY 5: BRICKS

Christmas can be a culturally challenging time to be a Christian. It's hard to find the right balance between all the bumper stickers out there. Are we supposed to Keep Christ in Christmas or are we supposed to remember that Jesus is the Reason for the Season? Are we supposed to buy Starbucks when the cups are green, but not red AND green? What about when the cups are white? Is it an ancient pagan practice to hang stockings for our children and wait for Santa Claus? Should we be furiously baking Happy Birthday Jesus cakes? Are we selling out if we wish our atheist friend "Happy Holidays," or are we being obnoxious if we say "Merry Christmas," when they so clearly do not celebrate it?

Those are just small examples. We all know that Christmas can be fraught with emotions that are strung tighter than twinkle lights around the banister. Sometimes the struggles of life are further amplified during the forced cheer and chores of the holidays. And, apologies to Joel Osteen and Oprah, but we are not guaranteed to live our best life now. In fact, 2 Corinthians 4:17-18 says, "Our troubles are small. They last only for a short time. But they are earning for us a glory that will last forever. It is greater than all our troubles."

In other words, our best life is yet to come.

This world is broken, and sometimes when we ask God to help us with a specific struggle He says wait. He does so because in His divine plan and power He knows exactly the right set of circumstances to glorify His name through our lives. God knows His plan, but, at least in the short run, we don't. That can be frustrating.

That frustration hit Moses like a ton of bricks during his first encounter with Pharaoh in Exodus 5. He and Aaron went before Pharaoh and said *exactly* what God told them to say. What could possibly go wrong? Well for starters, Pharaoh had a giant temper tantrum. Instead of being reasonable, he told the Israelites that they had to make just as many bricks as before, but now without being given straw.

I'm not a brick maker, but as I understand it, straw is a key ingredient for efficient brick making. So this was a big problem. It made brick making almost impossible; and yet, they had to do it. Their lives depended on it. On top of all that, Pharaoh called them lazy!

The foreman of the Israelites was beside himself and of course took it all out on Moses. He told him that this latest mandate from Pharaoh was all Moses' fault. Great start to the new job right? On his first day of being The Rescuer of God's People, Moses made everything basically terrible.

But let's just double check here… was God put off by this new demand to make bricks without straw?

This is the same God who spoke and a universe was created. The same God who turned dust into a man. The same God who would knock over entire city walls with the sound of a trumpet just 40 years later. The same God who would turn water into wine and who would turn four loaves of bread into enough to feed 5,000 people.

This is the God who is Jesus, and Jesus was born so that someday He would turn death into life.

Strawless bricks… not a big deal to God. Still, He didn't fix the problem right away. And He won't always fix our problems quickly either. Sometimes it will be hard. Sometimes when we follow God it will actually be much harder. Maybe it will be this Christmas. But Jesus said in John 16:33, "In this world you will have trouble. But be encouraged! I have won the battle over the world."

Knowing that God has a plan that ends with our lives being eternally safe and filled with ultimate joy can help us wade through the tinsel, the glitter, and the forced fa-la-la to see the real reason to celebrate Christmas. Even though we don't always see the answers, or know how to make our bricks without straw, Jesus does.

And the good news is that the biggest transformation that God does has nothing to do with straw and bricks anyway. It has to do with us. If we follow Jesus, He takes our broken lives and turns them into new lives, new creations that can not be broken again.

It was true then, and it's true now. For you, and for me.

Esther C. Baird

DAY 6: PROMISE

At Christmas time promises flutter from our lips as sweetly as sugar plum fairies. "I promise I'll show up to your Christmas party… I may just run a little bit late!" "I promise I won't roll my eyes, or even make a huffy sigh, when your Uncle starts talking politics." "I promise I LOVE this sweater; it's so… unique!" "I promise I'll be soooo good if I can get a new Nerf Gun Strong Arm Blaster for Christmas!"

(Side note: parents, don't fall for the Nerf gun trap. You will never, and I mean NEVER, find all the Nerf darts and discs. Then you'll have to buy more, and you will also never find those. Pretty soon your house will be 75% Nerf and there's really no coming back from that.)

And while those are some of the easier promises, we all know there are other promises that come around Christmas that are deeper, heart-issue, promises. Sometimes we keep them. Sometimes we don't. Sometimes we can't.

This is a broken world and we don't always, can't always, get it right. Sometimes we want so badly to keep a promise that we're simply not equipped to. Sometimes we let sin get in the way. And sometimes we feel forced to make a promise that was never ours to make. Promises are important, and when promises are not kept, it's natural to feel betrayed and angry.

When Moses realized the whole brick and straw situation was going badly, he forgot God's promise to him and complained to God, "Why, Lord? Why have you brought trouble on these people? Is this why you sent me?" (Exodus 5:22)

But God replied by reminding Moses that He was doing exactly what He'd said He'd do way back with Abraham. "You will know that I am the LORD your God when I throw off the load the Egyptians have put on your shoulders. *I will bring you to the land I promised with an oath to give to Abraham, Isaac and Jacob.* I lifted up my hand and promised it to them. The land will belong to you. I am the LORD." (Exodus 6:7-8, emphasis mine)

Another way of saying this is, "Everything is going exactly as I promised it would."

Now Moses didn't have a copy of Genesis to read because, well, he hadn't written it yet. But the Ancient Near East had a culture of oral tradition. So God's promises were not uttered a few hundred years earlier and then forgotten. No, they were handed down from generation to generation. And what God promised to Abraham, later recorded in Genesis 15:13-16, is that Abraham's offspring would live in a land that wasn't theirs, and they'd be slaves there. But then God would rescue them and be their God and bring them into the land He had shown to Abraham.

Here it was: Moses, no longer the baby in the little ark basket, was living smack in the middle of the fulfillment of God's promises. Even more exciting, God had given Moses a major role to play in His plan. But not as major as that other baby who would be born a few thousand years later. God had made other promises--promises which that baby would fulfill. Promises that built on the work He was doing with the Israelites. And guess who is living smack in the middle of God's fulfillment of those promises?

That's right, we are.

That second baby, Jesus, grew up and promised His people, those who follow Him as their Savior and King, that He was going to leave so He could prepare a place for them. He said, "There are many rooms in my Father's house. If this were not true, would I have told you that I am going there? Would I have told you that I would prepare a place for you there? If I go and do that, I will come back. And I will take you to be with me. Then you will also be where I am." (John 14:2-3)

Not just a promised land, but a promised room in God's house with Jesus.

This Christmas you are living in the middle of the biggest promise fulfillment of all time; and God won't break His promises. If you are a child of His promises, then this is happening to you, and for you. This is for real!

What Moses did getting the Israelites out of Egypt is small potatoes compared to what Jesus is doing now, every day, in our hearts and lives and in our world to get us ready to enter our promised land some day!

It was true for Moses and the Israelites, and it's true for us today. Then and now. For you, and for me.

DAY 7: PLAGUE

Here as we approach the actual exodus of Exodus, we must begin with that well loved Christmas story of the ten plagues. You know, swarming frogs, a river of blood, boils, death, and oh, please pass the eggnog.

No? Ok, perhaps the ten plagues, while famous, are not always the first thing we think of this time of year. Though, here in modern America we are not without our own Christmas plagues. Mariah Carey's *All I Want for Christmas* anyone? Elf on the Shelf? I mean cut me a giant tinsel covered break. I'm supposed to secretly pose a deranged looking toy elf around the house so my girls can go find him? And these poses should include cleverly staged messes to show what a mischievous elf he is? Newsflash: I have two actual living children, not to mention two actual living giant dogs, who with full transparency create messes all around the house. The very last thing I am going to do this Christmas is contribute to the chaos level of the house.

Alright, I admit it. It's possible we're dealing with slightly different sorts of plagues in Exodus.

What we need to see is that the plagues of Egypt were not as much about the people who were being afflicted, but about their gods. Egypt was the superpower of the day, and they had thousands of gods. Jeopardy watchers all know Ra was the sun god and chief deity. Anubis, the god of death was also high in the pantheon. Pharaoh himself claimed to be the god of the people reigning over their activities and work, making for the popular family motto: Don't mess with Pharaoh.

Each of the plagues tested the strength of the Israelites' God against the Egyptian pantheon of gods and their cycle of life and death. Their life source was the Nile which in turn watered their crops which then fed their livestock which supported the people who, when they died, were mummified and sent back to the gods. God's ten plagues went after these fundamental aspects of life and put their gods to the test.

Was this God, who had given His name as Yahweh, or I AM, really more powerful than the most powerful nation and gods on the planet? Plague, by plague, by plague, the answer was a resounding yes. God used the plagues to attack and devastate all areas of Egyptian life that were supposedly protected by their gods. The Nile, their source of life, turned to blood; their crops were ravaged by locusts; their livestock all died, and eventually their hope for the future died when God sent the angel of death to kill their firstborn.

God came to rescue His people and show the whole world that there was only one God with real power and authority. A divine warrior, God took on the powers of the day and won decisively, saying, "I will judge *all* the gods of Egypt. I am the Lord." (Exodus 12:12, emphasis mine)

God showed the world that He was in the business of overthrowing any other power that threatened His sovereign authority or His chosen people. That's why the plagues are a perfect Christmas story, because at Christmas we see Him do this again in an even bigger way.

Jesus was born to fight the ultimate battle against a power that threatened both God's authority and His chosen people. Jesus came to battle the power of sin in this world, and in our hearts. The angel Gabriel told Mary, "You will become pregnant and give birth to a son. You must call him Jesus. He will be great and will be called the Son of the Most High God. The Lord God will make him a king like his father David of long ago. The Son of the Most High God will rule forever over his people. They are from the family line of Jacob. That kingdom will never end." (Luke 1:31-33)

Egypt ended. The Roman rule of Jesus' time ended. Some day America will end. But Jesus? He is, and will always be, ruling forever. Jesus came to win the war with sin and to triumph over death. We know how this cosmic war ends, but there are still skirmishes and fights along the way. We still fight against the things that plague our hearts and our souls. Sometimes at Christmas we can feel those battles waging with heightened strength. Sometimes we feel like our security is being stripped away just as the plagues stripped Egypt.

But on that first Christmas, Jesus, the Son of God, our divine warrior king, came into our world to fight our battles for us. He has promised us that the war has long since been decided.

So yes, the plagues are a Christmas story. They point us to the ultimate battle and the ultimate reality that Jesus is reigning victorious on His throne forever--even now as you read this. And no matter what happens in our lives and in our world, He cannot be dethroned. There is no other deity or power, not even sin and death itself, that can win against Him.

No matter what plagues assail us this Christmas, if we follow Jesus, the baby of Bethlehem and our risen victorious warrior king, we are secure in His victory. It was true for the Israelites then, and it's true now. For you, and for me.

DAY 8: BONES

One of my favorite movies is *The Pirates of the Caribbean.* I love Johnny Depp's role as Captain Jack Sparrow and the swashbuckling fun of it all set to a great soundtrack. Argh, me matey and all that.

But one scene in the movie always gives me chills. (Spoiler alert: this will give away a plot twist, though, um, this movie has been out since 2003 so you might want to hop to it if you ever plan to see it.) It's the scene when the pirates are yo-ho-hoing on their ship with the recently captured Ms. Swan. As she is running about looking disheveled and horrified in a most stunning way, the moonlight falls on the pirates, revealing that they are skeletons. They looked alive and even seemed alive to themselves, but when the light shone on them... the truth was revealed. They were actually dead men--walking skeletons.

Does that resonate with you at all this Christmas? Do you ever feel like you're going through the motions? Sure, you're doing your job, talking to your family and friends, commuting every day, making dinners, going to kid's games, and generally acting like a person who is alive, but secretly do you feel emotionally or spiritually dead?

That night of the tenth plague on Egypt, every firstborn son, and some commentators speculate firstborn daughters, of any age, looked alive, but they were already skeletons. The angel of death was on the way and there was nothing anyone could do to stop it. The death sentence was already decided. By the light of morning, their true condition would be revealed. Death was the final plague.

Sometimes we feel that same death sentence. One of the great prophets, Ezekiel, was given a vision of this very thing. He says God put him down in a valley and "It was full of bones... I saw a huge number of bones in the valley. The bones were very dry." (Ezekiel 37:1-2) A whole valley full of skeletons. Dusty, dry, dead. In our culture we try to ignore our skeletons with our business, our fitness, our money, our education. Whatever "it" is, we pursue it--trying to prove that we're living, we're fine, we're great! But there is no business or education or achievement that could wake those skeletons up in Ezekiel's valley, or that could save those firstborn of Egypt.

Or us. Except...

There is a way out of the death we feel crumbling our bones into dust. After Ezekiel saw the piles of skeletons lying there, God told him to say, "Dry bones, listen to the Lord's message. The Lord and King speaks to you. He says, 'I will put breath in you. Then you will come to life again.'" (Ezekiel 37:4-5)

We can come to life again. It was foreshadowed in Egypt on that long night, when the angel of death passed over the Israelite homes that had been marked with the blood of a lamb, and it was completed in Bethlehem when Jesus, the Lamb of God, came to Earth.

If you feel like a walking skeleton, if this holiday season is confirming that your life is dusty or hard or as lifeless as dry bones, you need to stop hiding from the light. You need to get out of the darkness where your skeleton looks like a living person, and let the light expose your broken dry bones.

John's gospel explains that the birth of Jesus was the ultimate answer to the angel of death. He says when Jesus was born, "Life was in Him, and that life was the light for all people. The light shines in the darkness. But the darkness has not overcome the light." (John 1:1-4) When Jesus shines His light, the light of life, onto your dusty heart He exposes it. And then He saves it.

He takes your skeletal set of bones and gives you His light and His life and promises that darkness can never overcome you. Never.

It was true for the Israelites then, and it's true now. For you and for me.

DAY 9: LAMB

True confession: it's not really Christmas right now. I'm writing this advent book in the summer at the Silver Bay YMCA Conference Center on the shores of Lake George in upstate NY. My family has a cabin about a mile away, and Silver Bay is a big part of our daily routine. We take classes, sail Sunfish, get ice cream, do archery and generally enjoy summer, but... not without our badges. Every person who comes on campus, whether a week-long renter, a summer program member, or a kid in a youth group, has to wear a badge. The color of the badge indicates your membership level and allows you access to various parts of the campus.

One of my favorite days each year is when we get our badges for the summer. I am that annoying mom who makes our two daughters jump in the air while holding their badges so I can take a picture. I title it "Badges! It must be summer!" or some equally chirpy post that I'm sure will win me no creativity points. But our badges identify us and give us access to all the fun of Silver Bay.

Followers of Jesus have a badge too, and we can best understand it by going back to Egypt. That night of the tenth plague, there was one way, and one way only, that the angel of death would pass by your house, and it was through the visible sign, the badge, of the blood of a lamb on the door. No sign--no "badge"--meant no promise of life, and no access to God's victory over death.

But why? Was it magic lamb's blood? Did it work for wizards, but not for muggles? (Sorry if you're not a Harry Potter fan; you're wrong--but we can still be friends.) Of course not. It was a sign. An outward sign that said "this house and those in it belong to Yahweh." The Israelites followed God's very precise instructions as detailed in Exodus 12, and carried out that first Passover feast knowing that the lamb they killed not only provided the feast, but that its blood became the sign on the door that the family was to be spared.

God couldn't spell it out any more clearly. He didn't want His people to die. But in this broken and fallen world, we can't dwell with God or be part of His feast without dealing with our own sin. Our sin makes us unable to be with God; it actually kills us as surely as the angel of death killed the firstborn.

But God provided a way out. That night in Egypt, each family was allowed to substitute the sacrifice of a lamb for their lives. The lamb would die, and its blood would be the sign that in that house sin had been dealt with, at least for that night. The sacrificed lamb was not the ultimate answer, and the Israelites had to keep sacrificing a lamb every Passover. For years. And decades. And centuries. And millennia.

Until... Christmas.

Jesus came to be the final lamb that had to die. John the Baptist knew this, and when he saw Jesus about to start His ministry he said, "Look! The Lamb of God! He takes away the sin of the world!" (John 1:29)

The lambs of the Exodus each saved one family for one night as the angel of death passed over. The Lamb of God came to save each person from their sins and to give victory over spiritual death for those who followed Him--for all of time.

If we follow that Lamb, we don't have to paint our houses with blood, because we have a new sign that should be visible to all who see it. The very Spirit of God lives in us, and "the fruit the Holy Spirit produces is love, joy and peace. It is being patient, kind and good. It is being faithful and gentle and having control of oneself." (Galatians 5:22-23) Those who know us should see the fruits of the Spirit in our words, our actions, our lives. It should be the biggest, brightest, most colorful badge we can wear.

Let your friends, your family, your neighbors, your coworkers see that you are saved from death, for all time. The proof is in how you live your life, perhaps especially during this high stress time of year.

Jesus the Passover Lamb paid the price for our lives. It was foreshadowed for the Israelites on that first Passover, and it has become eternally, fully true for us now at Christmas. Jesus came to be our Lamb. He came for you, and for me.

Esther C. Baird

DAY 10: LOST

I love the Fall. It's one of the reasons I started going over-the-top-bananas at Christmas. After all the foliage and crisp lovely air and pumpkin spiced lattes, the early winter is just too gross to endure without extreme decorations. But one thing about the Fall makes the wheels come straight off my wagon. I give you: The Corn Maze.

You know how many times I have enjoyed wandering around a field of corn where the bugs are plentiful and the snacks and bathrooms are not? Never! Not a single time has it been fun. One time we were doing a corn maze with our two daughters and my sister-in-law. We'd been trudging and getting nowhere for longer than infinity. Ok, maybe an hour. But there was nowhere for our youngest to go potty; I couldn't find any snacks to appease my eldest; and my sister-in-law was in high heeled boots that, while stylish, did not lend themselves to the occasion. We were mid-maze and deeply, deeply lost.

I was not having it. I was a grown adult in modern America, and I was not spending one more minute with young children on the verge of meltdown and a sister-in-law who was going to develop gangrene if she took another step.

I studied the position of the sun and then charged

directly through the corn maze walls to where I knew good and well the parking lot was. A stunned corn maze attendant called after us, "There's only one way out!" I barked back, "Trust me, there is more than one way!" and out we emerged.

While I'm sure that you, my sensible readers, would handle that specific situation with more grace than I did, in life we all sometimes feel lost. And even if we flip out, we still may have no idea where we are going.

You can imagine that the suddenly free Israelites, after 400 years of slavery, had no idea where they were going either. There was this vague sense of heading back to the land of their forefathers, this land that God had promised them. But how? Where? The answer came in a most unexpected way. After they escaped on the night of the Passover, the Bible says, "By day the Lord went ahead of them in a pillar of cloud. It guided them on their way. At night he led them with a pillar of fire. It gave them light. So they could travel by day or at night." (Exodus 13:21)

To be clear, God didn't just send a cloud; He inhabited the cloud as a sign that He was right there with them. And at night, He didn't just send fire, He showed himself to His people through the fire. Both the cloud and the fire demonstrated God's great power and strength.

But most of all God was saying that His people would not be lost. He would show them exactly where to go so that their path would be clear. The Israelites took 40 years to get to the Promised Land. God wasn't promising them a short journey; He was just promising that He would lead them and be with them if they followed Him.

I think we all would love a pillar of fire to come down from heaven and make it clear where we should go. This job or that job? Move to a new neighborhood or stay put? Just follow the big flaming pillar south down the interstate, and when it lands at a school, send your kids there.

Actually, we have something better. When Jesus was born at Christmas, He came not as a giant flaming pillar or a huge cloud full of wind and power. He was a newborn infant. A small, fragile baby. But this baby grew up to say, "I am the way and the truth and the life." (John 14:6)

Jesus shows us the way, and while we may not always know exactly which road to travel in this life, we can trust that as long as we are following Jesus, He will direct our path. Proverbs 3:6 says, "In all your ways obey him. Then he will make your paths smooth and straight."

If you are a child of God's promises, then you are never lost. You have a perfect guide dwelling within you, directing your way, and ultimately leading you to the promised land just as He did for the Israelites. It was true then and it's true now. For you, and for me.

DAY 11: WATER

The story of the Israelites crossing the Red Sea is probably the most popular image of the Exodus narrative. What really happened is also fiercely debated in the world of ancient history studies. Should you find yourself at an archeology happy hour, maybe don't mention the crossing if you want to get out before bedtime. I've read a lot of articles about the exact location of the Red Sea, or whether we should we call it the Sea of Reeds, and when exactly it could have occurred if all things were equal. (Although, in my mind, any time God supernaturally parts a large body of water, things aren't equal.) I also once spent half a summer teasing out exactly what it meant that the waters piled up in a "heap," as Moses described in Exodus 15. I can tell you a lot about the grammatical history of the word "heap" as used in ancient flood narratives. It's possible that wasn't my most socially exciting summer.

For our purposes we're going to just acknowledge that the Red Sea crossing was the original light and water show, and God used the event to save His people and to destroy Pharaoh's.

We read a few days ago about how we were as good as skeletons until Jesus came as our sacrificial lamb to give us new life. And we read way back on Day 1 that water, in the ancient world, often symbolized death. (There wasn't a strong local YMCA yet to train up those guppies and minnows.) Here on Day 11 we put it all together.

God is a Holy God who demands payment for all our sins, past, present and future. And He receives payment in the form of the sacrificial lamb--both the ones at Passover in Egypt, and through Jesus once and for all in our lives.

But something beyond Jesus dies. The good news is that it's us. At least our sinful self. Romans 6:8 says, "Now if we died with Christ, we believe that we will also live with Him." The writer, Paul, was referring to that deep down darkness that we are born with. It's sin, and when Jesus died He took all of our brokenness into death with Him.

God used Moses to illustrate this concept by leading the Israelites across the Red Sea in Exodus 14. God quite literally took certain death, looming, deadly water piled (or heaped) up high enough that all of Pharaoh's army drowned in it, and God created a path through it for His people to life on the other side.

This necessary path through death is the only way to life on the other side. It's the path Isaiah described in chapter 43:2 when he prophesied, "When you pass through the waters I will be with you."

We have no Red Sea around here. I live near the ocean, but church membership does not require us to part the Atlantic (though that might improve our lobster intake). Thankfully, instead of parting seas, we get baptized. And when we do, we are symbolizing (whether you dunk or sprinkle) this very act of going into water, into death, and coming out the other side with new life.

We are doing symbolically what Jesus came at Christmas to do in reality. In a way we are re-enacting crossing the Red Sea by remembering that Jesus allowed the waters of death to completely engulf Him. His whole life's work led up to that point. When He went down into death He stayed there for three long days. But when He overthrew death and resurrected, He wasn't just alive again, He also fully paid for life, eternal life, for all of those who follow Him.

Again Paul wrote, "By being baptized, we were buried with Christ into His death. Christ has been raised from the dead by the Father's glory. And like Christ we also can live a new life." (Romans 6:4)

Christmas can be a time when the waters start to pile up on either side. Perhaps you feel a looming sense of them hemming you in. Our culture would like to tell us that our big fancy Egyptian chariots that are state of the art, or our shiniest royal educations and degrees, or being a member of the favored circles with the most prestige can get us across the waters before they crash down. But none of those things, not one of them, will get to the other side. They all will be sent to the bottom of the waters where they rot. Even the Lexus in those annoying Christmas commercials. It's super pretty, but it's going to sink.

Only the living get to the other side. And we can only live when we grab hold of Jesus and follow Him through death and onward toward life eternal.

Are we willing to let God take our sinful nature and wash it away? If we are children of God's promises, then the other side awaits; it's dry and it's firm. Jesus stands there saying He has made a way across, through death, through Him, and on to ultimate safety.

He led His people across to dry land then, and He leads us now. He does it for you, and for me.

Esther C. Baird

DAY 12: CAROL

Each week at the church where I work we have a mid-week staff meeting, and we often talk about the upcoming Sunday service. As we approach advent, I always suggest that we sing Christmas hymns, every Sunday, every song. I want Christmas hymns all December with no exceptions! Other staff, specifically those who are actually gifted in music and worship, will suggest we introduce a new song, or a variation on a theme. While they tend to win out, since they know what they are doing, I stick to my Christmas guns. I want to sing Christmas hymns, and only Christmas hymns, from Thanksgiving through New Years. No moderation!

It's possible that I annoy a lot of people around Christmas time.

Regardless of my preferences, people do love to sing at Christmas to celebrate and to enjoy songs about the birth of Jesus--the amazing, giant, universe-bending event that came in the form of a pretty dicey birth story. We sing because it's in our tradition to do so. Our earliest Christmas carols, still popular today, date back to the mid-1700's, but, of course, there were earlier ones. There is even one, let's call it a pre-Christmas carol, found in Exodus 15. It's called the song of Moses.

Maybe as a child you sang this at your local VBS, so the first few words will be familiar, especially if you sang in the King James version, which, if you were a VBS child of the 70's or 80's, you did. Feel free to do the hand motions as you read along: "I will sing unto the Lord, for He hath triumphed gloriously: the horse and his rider he hath thrown into the sea." (KJV, Exodus 15:1)

Moses went on to describe how God rescued His people out of Egypt and would continue to deliver them as they made their way toward the promised land.

Moses said two things of note as we consider it from our Christmas carol point of view. First he said, "Because your love is faithful, you will lead the people you have set free," and secondly he declared, "You will bring them in. You will plant them on the mountain you gave them. Lord, you have made that place your home." (Exodus 15:13, 17)

This was true for Israel as they were freed from Egypt, as they headed to Mount Sinai, and later as they built the temple on the mount in Jerusalem. But it is also true for us today, because we've been set free by Jesus, and God makes His home in our very hearts.

Moses sang the first Christmas song and it foreshadowed the next Christmas song, which was also sung before Jesus was born, but much, much closer to His birth. It was sung by His mother, Mary. Mary said that God had done great things for her and that His name was holy. She went on to say, "His mercy is for those who fear him from generation to generation." (NIV, Luke 1:50)

Well here we are, many, many, many generations later. A people set free. A people who can dwell with God. A people for whom God has done great things, and a people who receive His mercy.

We are people from different periods in time, under different circumstance, but we sing one song, an eternal song. The song is always about God's plan to make a way that we can be with Him. The song is always about Jesus. I like to think of it as the Christmas carol that never ends.

In fact, in Revelation when we see a vision of our eternal promised land to come, Scripture says, "They sang the song of God's servant Moses and of the Lamb." (Revelation 15:3)

It is a song that was true when Moses first sang it; it was true when Mary sang her version; it's true today, and it will always be true. God has triumphed gloriously. Then and now. For you, and for me.

Esther C. Baird

DAY 13: CARD

If you are reading this on schedule, it's mid-December. I'm going to ask you a question that will either make you smug or panicked. Have you sent out your Christmas cards yet?

Either you're overly organized and did it back in August, which was so amazing of you but actually makes me think you should take me off your list because we may not relate to each other that well, or you haven't even taken a photo of your family yet and may just draw some stick figures, post it to Facebook, and call it a win. Or perhaps you've chosen a third option and skipped Christmas cards altogether. You've gone rogue. You're confident your family exists without proving it in a photo, and you are officially my hero.

In the end, I send cards every year because I know it's about relationships. Maybe not with my friends I see every day; they just laugh at my card. "Look, Esther wore an outfit and did her hair! Must be the Christmas card!" Rather, my cards are for long distance family, my new friends, my husband's co-workers, and our veterinarian. (Trust me, he deserves an entire Christmas parade for the nonsense he puts up with because of our two Bernese Mountain Dogs.) Christmas cards are a way of connecting to people, to say you remember them and value them... and possibly to show that you can color coordinate your family for one nano-second each year.

Over the next few days we are going to look at something that gets a lot of bad press, but actually is perhaps the original Christmas card, way before there was even a baby-in-a-manger-stamp to buy. Way before the baby was even born.

I'm talking about the Ten Commandments.

Really? Those rules everyone is always fighting about hanging or not hanging in the state capitals? That list of thou shalts and thou shalt nots? They aren't remotely Christmasy, are they?

Oh yes… they are very much Christmasy.

The Ten Commandments, as God gave them to Moses in Exodus 20, began an amazing portion of Scripture where God came to Moses on Mount Sinai and interacted with him, spoke with him, and told him what He required of us in order to be in relationship with Him.

Moses didn't call them the Ten Commandments by the way. Moses introduced the Ten Commandments by saying, "Here are all the *words* God spoke." (Exodus 20:1, emphasis mine.) And then the Ten Commandments follow.

Remember another time God spoke some words? For example, some words in the beginning? "And God said…" and all creation happened. When God speaks words, it's not like us chit-chatting at the coffee shop. When God speaks words, things are created, life happens, love and truth and mercy happen. All that is and all that will ever be happens because of God's words.

God knew His people needed guidance; they'd been under Egyptian rule for 400 years. And let's face it, we still need guidance just as much today. While books and commentaries and entire libraries have been written about what it means to be in relationship with God, He summed it all up--guided the Israelites and us--in ten words. God gave us His words to reach across space and time and our very natures so that we could have a relationship with Him.

It's the first Christmas card.

Ten life giving, heart changing, words from God. Ten words that point to another Word who would come in person, who would embody all that God's words ever were or would mean, because this Word would be God. This Word was Jesus, as John makes super clear when he opens his gospel. "In the beginning, the Word was already there. The Word was with God, and the Word was God." (John 1:1)

This Word would show us how to live out the Ten Commandments to the fullest. Jesus, the Word, would show us how to perfectly be in relationship with God. But before we visit the baby, the ultimate Christmas gift, the Word, in the manger, we need to understand those ten words God spoke and how He spoke them.

Plus, if you still haven't done your Christmas cards, you now have my permission to simply send out a copy of the Ten Commandments, maybe with a cute green and red border. I'm sure it will be a big hit.

But first, take out your copy (they're in Exodus 20), because this week we're going to take a closer look at how God spoke to the Israelites then, and how He still speaks to us now. Desiring a relationship with you, and with me.

Esther C. Baird

DAY 14: MOUNTAIN

I like to hike in a day-trip sort of way. But ask my family about it, and they will likely roll their eyes. I'm known for picking day hikes that should, in theory, be easy, but somehow end up long, rugged and reminiscent of the Bataan Death March. Blood almost always makes an appearance. This has been true since I was a child. I never meant to get wedged on a cliff, or miles down a strange twisting road, but I have vivid childhood memories of being with my cousins in those very situations.

It only got worse. As my husband and I celebrated our first wedding anniversary, I planned a lovely hike that landed us in a downpour up above the tree line in the Smoky Mountains, wearing flip flops, with no food or water. It might have bee beautiful if there had been sun and if we weren't starving, freezing, and covered in blisters.

But who's complaining; we're alive. We lived to hike another day, and I'm not asking if you want to hike with me. I'm just telling you I like mountains, and I like to be on them.

In Exodus however, when God gave the law to Moses on Mount Sinai, it was a mountain that the people could not go near, or even approach. God said, "Be careful that you do not go near the mountain. Do not even touch the foot of it.

Whoever touches the mountain must be put to death." (Exodus 19:12)

That's a pretty clear "No Trespassing" sign. Stay away from the mountain.

Here's the conundrum: God was on the mountain. God literally came down onto the mountain in smoke and fire and thunder as He had been doing by day and by night while leading the people. He came onto the mountain to give Moses His ten words--His words designed to tell people how they could be in a right relationship with Him. But the people could go nowhere near Him.

It's worth remembering that the last time people could freely be with God was in the Garden of Eden. Adam and Eve lived with God, and it was fine--it was good. It was fine, of course, until they sinned and broke the relationship. Ever since then, our sin is totally and completely antithetical to all God is, and our sin makes approaching Him a death sentence. Then, as now, we were designed to be with God; it's our deepest longing, but we dare not approach the mountain.

God is holy and the Israelites were not. They were complainers and whiners and deceitful and untrusting. In sum, they were just like us. They were under the same sentence of death that we are.

We feel an impassable chasm between what we are and what we were meant for. Probably a lot of us feel it a little more during this time of year. And yet, also during this time of year, we remember that God wants to be in relationship with us so much that He allowed His own Son to be born and then carry all of our guilt and sin and anger and fear and deceit.

If you go up the mountain, if you enter into God's presence with any bit of sin, let alone the sin of the world, you die. And Jesus was born as both God and man in order to do just that. Jesus came to touch the mountain because

He was fully God, and to touch it with our sin because He was fully man, and then to accept the penalty for our sin and die.

In doing so, we see that Jesus provided us access to the mountain. Someday we will be on God's mountain with no danger and no fear. Isaiah shows us what that will be like: "On that mountain the Lord will destroy the veil of sadness that covers all the nations. He will destroy the gloom that is spread over everyone. He will swallow up death forever. The Lord and King will wipe away the tears from everyone's face." (Isaiah 25:6-8)

No more sadness. No more gloom. No more death. No more tears. That is the reality that God promises for His people on His mountain with Him. This Christmas, whether you have a family hike or not in your future, you can know that you can approach the mountain, because Jesus approached it first and is inviting you to follow.

It was true then, and it's true now. For you, and for me.

DAY 15: GOD

Christmas can bring out the better, more loving sides of our personality or, perversely, do just the opposite. By the time the Christmas tree has fallen over (twice), and the dog has shredded the nicely wrapped gifts, and your aunt insists on helping in the kitchen, which you know means something is going to catch on fire, patience may not only be long gone, but *you* may actually be long gone, too.

So, as the "ho ho ho" wears thin, what better time could there be than the fraught Christmas season to discuss a set of words from God that tells us how to relate to Him, and to all parts of our lives--even that crazy aunt? Are we really, I mean REALLY, supposed to follow the Ten Commandments these many thousands of years later? Did Jesus actually care about them? Couldn't they just be sort of a Moses era thing? Nope. In fact, Jesus makes this abundantly clear in Matthew 5. During the famous Sermon on the Mount, Jesus said it's not just enough to smugly say you haven't murdered a person, but He taught that if you've even been angry with a person you've committed murder in your heart.

Ever been angry with a person? That's a rhetorical question; no need to answer.

The Commandments are not limited to just the words given to Moses; they include all the variety of ways they are expressed in our lives--in thought and deed. So perhaps on a given day you didn't tell a bold-faced lie. Fabulous! But don't tweet everyone just yet, because any time you misrepresent something or someone (including yourself), any time you boast or you gossip or you omit, you are breaking the ninth Commandment about lying. The Commandments also represent the flip side--not just "shall not" but "shall." It's not enough to not lie, but you must also speak the truth at all times. Speak truth into all conversations, all thoughts, and at all places including work and home.

Ever gossip? Ever brag? Um...

This feels exhausting, especially at Christmas. It feels like a big old set-up for failure, and there is already enough of that to go around this season.

It gets worse.

The Commandments are listed in such a way that if you can't keep the first one, you automatically are going to fail at the next nine. The first Commandment is "Do not put any other gods in place of me." (Exodus 20:3)

Now, before we think about what that means, consider this. In Matthew 22, Jesus was asked a bunch of trick questions by the Pharisees to try to trip Him up. Except... He's Jesus, so the trick backfired. When they asked Him to pick which of all the Commandments was the greatest, it was a set-up. What would He do? What would He say?

He didn't choose. Instead He summarized. He said the greatest Commandment was to "'Love the Lord your God with all your heart and with all your soul. Love him with all your mind.' This is the first and most important commandment. And the second is like it. 'Love your neighbor as you love yourself.' Everything that is written in the Law and the Prophets is based on these two commandments." (Matthew 22:37-40)

That was the summary of all the Law, the Ten Commandments as well as all of the laws in the Old Testament. Scholars believe there were 601 of them. And here's the interesting thing: when God gave Moses the Ten Commandments, they were divided into two types. The first four Commandments were about how we treat God, and the remaining six were about how we treat each other.

Sound familiar? Love God, love people. You may have seen it on a wooden script sign or in an Instagram post with a pretty sunset behind it. It may be pithy and short, but it's anything but simple.

When you begin to consider the full implications of that one statement, you realize really, really fast that you are way out of your league.

The very first of the Ten Commandments sets the stage for how we are to be in relationship with God. It might be tempting to think this was only written to the Israelites who had just left Egypt with its large cast of deities. Perhaps, they needed a crash course on monotheism.

But aside from other major religions, we don't believe in a lot of different gods here in America, right? So what's the problem?

Not so fast. Remember the variety of ways the Commandments can be expressed. Remember the flip side of the Commandments. If your first priority in life is anything other than following, loving, and obeying God, the one true God, then you are breaking the first Commandment and probably all the rest. If you can't be in a right relationship with God, you are certainly not in a right relationship with people. The one precedes the other.

How often do we secretly think that if we just marry the right kind of person, or get the right job, or have recognition for a certain success, or make certain people happy, or feel especially healthy, we'll actually be happy, feel fulfilled and think we've got it all together? If you think this is all you need, then they are your idols, your god. Oops.

When God gave His law to Moses, He knew it would be beyond our ability to follow or keep. He knew we'd be in trouble, and yet He still gave it, because He knew that ultimately the law would point us back to Him.

Jesus didn't wave off the law when He summarized the Commandments into two parts. They were the same two key requirements on which God built the Ten Commandments. Jesus didn't ignore the laws; He fulfilled them. He came at Christmas because the law showed how much we needed help--how impossible it was for us to ever be right with God and how much we needed grace.

Every day, every single minute, Jesus loves God the Father perfectly with all His heart and soul and mind. What's more, Jesus gives us His Spirit so that this perfect love is possible for us. We won't always get it right, but each day, if we follow Jesus, our love for God will grow into what we are designed and called to be: a people who love God and put nothing else in His place--even when it means loving your aunt who burned the Christmas meal.

This is what Jesus does for us, even now, even in December. He helps us love God because He is God. He was then, and He is now. And He does this for you, and for me.

DAY 16: PEOPLE

Since we solved all the problems yesterday surrounding putting God first and loving Him (or, you know, realized we can't solve anything at all) we can turn our attention to the second set of Commandments that have to deal with people.

I joke a lot about working in church ministry. I'm asked how I like it, and my standard line back is, "I love my job as long as I don't have to interact with any people!"

I get a lot of stares. But people can be super difficult to work with. They are annoying and opinionated and have weird idiosyncratic ideas. They are bossy and overly talkative, and think they are funnier than they actually are. Christians, in particular, carry a heavy backpack of theological dogma and historical baggage that informs everything from when they roll their eyes over hymn selections to their "biblically based" insistence on bringing coffee into the sanctuary.

I know, because that paragraph is a summary of me. Ask anyone I work with. I promise they will quickly agree with my assessment, and they may even want to add a few things. (Look, I don't care what anyone says or how new the carpet is, if I want to bring coffee into church on Sunday morning, which starts early, then I'm going to. It has a spill proof lid--I bought it after I spilled a cup that didn't have one. No, I do not need to reread yesterday's thoughts on idolatry.)

So when the second half of the Commandments is about loving people, any of us who interact with any people, *ever*, need to take notice.

Here's the tricky part about this second portion of the ten words from God. We're commanded to love people, got it. Later in Deuteronomy God commands more specifically that we are to love our neighbor as ourselves. As we saw yesterday, Jesus reiterates this in Matthew 22. But also, in Matthew 5:44 Jesus ratchets it up saying, "… here is what I tell you. Love your enemies. Pray for those who hurt you."

But… all people are broken. All annoying. All sinful. All capable of hurt and anger and harm.

If we love people, if we honor our parents, if we don't murder (even in our hearts), if we treat our neighbors as ourselves and according to the Commandments, we may still get hurt in return. Scratch that. We will get hurt.

At least in the first four Commandments, when we love God, we know He will always love us and respond to us perfectly, with holiness and justice, guided by perfect love, grace and mercy.

People, not so much.

It's hard to love people who may hurt us in return. It's hard to not think dark thoughts toward someone who wishes you ill or, perhaps worse, wishes someone you love ill.

This time of year, some of the relationships that are hardest for you may feel even harder. Perhaps you have a strained family relationship, and you don't talk. Well it's even more obvious when you don't talk during Christmas. If you are bitter about your boss's treatment of you, you are likely to feel even more bitter during Christmas when they make you work long hours and refuse to acknowledge that the rest of the country is celebrating.

It's not safe to love people, because they may return your love with harm.

Loving others may seem to be asking too much, yet the very thing that seems most oppressive about the Commandments is in fact the most freeing. We don't, we can't, we won't keep the Commandments perfectly or even well; but Jesus did. And if we follow Him, if He is our one true God, then we get to take His perfect track record as our own.

Because of that, it's possible to love other people. No matter what they do in response to our love, our identity is sealed up with Jesus. The apostle John mentioned our identity in Christ when he talked about the early days of Jesus' public ministry. John said, "Some did accept Him [Jesus]. They believed in His name. He gave them the right to become children of God." (John 1:12) Jesus brought us into His family.

Jesus keeps us safe. He guards our heart. He loves us perfectly. We are free to love others, even if they are unloving in response, because God first loved us when we were unloving.

This doesn't mean we need to be doormats to abuse or evil. We need to be on guard, perhaps especially in the church, that such things are not allowed and are called out at every turn. But it's also true that you are more capable of loving that bitter boss, that silent family member, that annoying church staff member if you do not base your love for them on their reaction. Instead, base your love for them on Jesus' love for you.

This Christmas you can love others. God commanded it to Moses way back on Mount Sinai, and Jesus reaffirmed it during His life on earth. It's a real Commandment that was true for them, and true for us. We can love people because God first loved us. We can love difficult people because their response does not define us; God defines us. He defined His people then, and He defines us now. Jesus' life, and the life He gives those who follow Him, proves that this is true for you, and for me.

DAY 17: CALF

One of the gifts I have is the ability to sit patiently in doctors' waiting rooms. Ok, not really. In fact, I'm terrible at it. I tap my foot loudly, I huff in a way that makes it clear why I'm huffing, and I whisper in my best stage whisper things like, "I'm so glad I pulled my child out of school so she could sit in this waiting room!"

It's not my most endearing quality, and over the years God has reminded me that doctors' waiting rooms are not a Fruits-of-the-Spirit-free-zone, and, pssst, patience is one of the fruits (see Galatians 5:22). This reminder once came in the form of the doctor saying "I'm sorry to keep you, we had an emergency that was life or death. But I'm sure your waiting was frustrating."

Whoops.

At Christmas, patience can be especially hard to come by. The lines in the stores are longer, the clerks are snappier, and the to-do lists are never ending. It's easy to think that if we could just do it our way, things would run better, faster, and more efficiently. But whether in small things or in large things, sometimes God has us wait, and reminds us that He is in control, not us.

While Moses was getting the law from God up on Mount Sinai, the Israelites had to wait. Somewhere in the weeks of waiting, they got huffy and impatient. They said to Aaron, "Come, make us gods who will go before us. As for this fellow Moses who brought us up out of Egypt, we don't know what has happened to him." (Exodus 32:2)

This fellow Moses? Did they mean the guy who led them out of the country that had oppressed them for 400 years; the guy who they knew full well was up on the mountain with God that very minute? Sure they knew what Moses was doing, but God's timing wasn't good enough. The people thought they could handle things better, faster, more efficiently. You can almost imagine them saying, "Let's make a god right now and get this thing done rather than wait for some God up on a mountain."

The story is well-known. Aaron asked them for their gold jewelry, melted it down and made a golden calf. He then told them, perhaps in his best stage whisper, that the golden calf was their god. They could stop waiting; they'd solved the problem themselves. Ta-da! We got this! Are we Israelites great or what!?

It would be a gross understatement to say that things went badly for that proud, impatient people. Things always go badly when we make our own gods and think our own answers are better than His.

Perhaps you aren't melting down your jewelry in a backyard bonfire, but we all are making our own gods when we try to be in charge, to manipulate relationships, or to trust in a career to provide our ultimate security. Any time we impatiently think we can handle our life better than God, we are making and bowing down to our own personal golden calf.

Like the Israelites, it will end badly. When Moses came down from Mount Sinai and saw what was going on, he ordered the death of nearly 3,000 people. And while we may survive the day when we make our own version of the calf, it's only because Jesus already died for us. There is only one

God. Remember that's the first Commandment, and anything short of loving and obeying God alone is idolatry, just as surely as if we put up a statue in our living room. And idolatry always, every single time, leads to death.

Here's the amazing part: at Christmas we actually celebrate that God knows about, and is not surprised by, our lumpy, melted down, home-made gods and idols.

God knew what was happening while He was talking to Moses. He knew that even as He gave Moses instructions about how His chosen people could live peacefully with Him, they were rebelling. And when Jesus came to earth, He knew that the very people He came to save would end up killing Him. He knew they wanted a king who would fix what *they* thought needed fixing.

All along our biggest problem has never been something out there; it has always been in us, in our hearts. No human king, or lump of gold, or perfect job, or brilliant child, or stellar education can fix our hearts. Only God can, and only God does. Even if we feel like it's too long, too complicated, too hard of a life, God is working. Even when we are impatient with how our lives are turning out, the Bible says, "The Lord is not slow in keeping his promises, as some understand slowness. Instead he is patient with you, not wanting anyone to perish, but everyone to come to repentance." (2 Peter 3:9)

God's timing is always for our benefit. It's always about giving people the chance to turn and follow Him. It's about giving us time to abandon the junk idols we have created so that in God's timing we can recognize that only Jesus can change what's broken; only Jesus can change our hearts.

God's plan is always perfect, even at this time of year when things seem so short of perfect and when we are tempted to impatiently stomp around and fix things ourselves.

God wants our hearts. He wanted the Israelites' hearts then, and He wants ours now. Jesus came knowing full well we'd still try to melt stuff down into lumps of control in our pride and impatience. That is the Christmas gift: that even though He knew us and our intentions, He came anyway to give us new hearts. A new heart for you, and for me.

DAY 18: FREEDOM

Every Christmas, Oprah releases a list of her 'Favorite Things'. When she had her talk show, she'd spend a full episode on her favorite brand of PJs, her favorite candle, her favorite mixed nut snack bag, her favorite television. On and on it would go. On and on it still goes. Even without the show, she still announces a list each year, and what follows is a wild frenzy. The items she selects sell out within hours. I've seen interviews with store owners who need to hire extra staff when Oprah picks their product. Websites crash and phone lines clog with people trying to buy an actual Oprah Christmas gift.

Sometimes it's fun to watch the list reveal and the people going crazy, but mostly I stare at it and feel exhausted. The media pushes us at Christmas to believe there is some perfect item, some amazing gadget or toy, that will demonstrate our love and thoughtfulness. Christmas is a giant measuring stick, and you better measure up. So get out there, get shopping or decorating or party planning so you can make "it" all happen. Sorry if the last thing you feel is joy or peace. Joy and peace look nice in a splashy font on a Christmas card, but they aren't for real people. Not in December. Try again.

But what if it was real? What if you could have true joy and true peace this Christmas?

While I know most people don't look at the Ten Commandments as a relief to the constant striving, that's what they are. They are your ticket out of the rat race.

Remember what Christmas is all about? The angel told the shepherds in very clear terms, "Do not be afraid. I bring you good news. It will bring great joy for all the people. Today in the town of David a Savior has been born to you. He is the Messiah, the Lord." (Luke 2:10-11)

Good news of great joy? It sure sounds better than anxiety and worry. But how? And what does this have to do with the law?

Everything. It has everything to do with the law.

Later in the New Testament we read in Galatians about what was actually happening that night in Bethlehem. The universe shifted, and Christmas should NEVER be about anything else. Because "Then the chosen time came. God sent his Son. A woman gave birth to him. He was born under the authority of the law. *He came to set free those who were under the authority of the law.* He wanted us to be adopted as children with all the rights children have. Because you are his children, God sent the Spirit of his Son into our hearts. He is the Holy Spirit. By his power we call God 'Abba.' Abba means Father. So you aren't a slave any longer. You are God's child. Because you are his child, God gives you the rights of those who are his children." (Galatians 4:4-7, emphasis mine)

That night when Jesus was born, it was all about the law. He was born under it, just as we are.

He was born under the law to buy our freedom. His perfect life of law-keeping, His death and His resurrection, all of it, was so that we do not need to feel dread and exhaustion and Christmas fatigue.

Instead we can rest (remember what rest is?) and know that if we follow that baby who was born under the law and grew to be the Messiah, then we are children of God. We are not children who need to cater to Oprah's lists. We are not children who need to achieve some standard every year on the family Christmas trip. We are not children who need to have the best teacher gifts and the perfect conversational banter at the office party. We are children of the King of the universe. We are children who hear the good news and, therefore, we have great joy.

Great, great joy. This is God's promise to us. The law, the Ten Commandments, God's words to us; they are an amazing gift because they bring us to Jesus. They bring us to freedom.

God designed us to be free to follow Him. Free to feel joy. Free to know certain peace. It was true for the Israelites when God gave them the law even if they did not fully know how it would all be accomplished, and it's true for us now because of Jesus.

It's good news this Christmas for you, and for me.

Esther C. Baird

DAY 19: BLUEPRINT

Ok, I know it's taboo to mention Dan Brown's *The DaVinci Code* in some church circles. Yes, he wrote an action novel based on the life of Jesus that ended up concluding He'd married Mary Magdalene. Yes, the novel uses the Gospel of Thomas as if it were a suppressed genuine book of the Bible. Yes, the book twists ancient church history, while playing close enough to the truth that it rings sort of plausible to fans of conspiracy theories.

But two things: first, the book is fiction and frankly it was a fun, if at times irritating, read; and second, any book that got that much media attention and hype means it was touching on something deeper in its readers. I think the book appealed to so many people because it gave them answers to some of life's big questions. Granted they were the wrong answers, but let's think about the correct ones.

A major part of the *DaVinci* plot was answered through clues built into buildings--specifically Paris' famous Louvre museum. Wouldn't that be handy? What if we could just look at a building, its architecture or the items placed within it, and understand the answers we needed in life?

For example, what if a building blueprint could help you decide what to get your picky family member for Christmas. What if it could show you how to pretend you attended the children's Christmas concert when in fact you were stuck late at work. What if it could settle the age old debate: are matching Christmas pajamas for the entire family a good or bad idea?

Though perhaps those aren't the burning questions you have this Christmas. Maybe you have deeper, harder, more complicated questions about your life, your purpose, or your status with God. What if you could find answers to those questions?

There was a building in Exodus that God designed that actually did provide answers in a way Dan Brown could never even dream of. Truth, in this case, was way more amazing than fiction.

The building (it was actually a tent), was the tabernacle that God commanded Moses to build beginning in Exodus 25.

The tabernacle? That section of the Bible with all the directions about build-this-out-of-that-wood, and measure-this-curtain-by-that-length? Isn't that a part of Scripture that most people skip? Yes, and by skipping it they miss the big clues. Just for starters, the very word tabernacle is the Hebrew word for 'dwell'. In biblical Hebrew you could say, "I want to come tabernacle with you," and that would make sense.

The tabernacle that God instructed Moses to build was an amazing blueprint that led straight to Christmas day, to the coming of Jesus, and to the work that He would do. The tabernacle, in all its detail, its specificity, its cubits of acacia wood and overlays of gold, signaled that God not only wanted to dwell with us, but that He would provide a way to do so.

We know this is true because when Jesus was born the Bible says,"The Word became flesh and dwelt [*tabernacled*] among us for a while." (John 1:14)

The New Testament book of Hebrews talks a lot about the tabernacle and calls everything that Moses built in Exodus a mere copy of the real thing. It was a way to begin to show the Israelites the answers God had in store for them. And now we don't need to look forward to the answers, because we have them. Jesus came at Christmas. He replaced the whole tabernacle structure with Himself. "Christ did not enter a sacred tent made with human hands. That tent was only a copy of the true one. He entered heaven itself. He did it to stand in front of God for us. He is there right now." (Hebrews 9:24)

Right now. Right now while Jesus is dwelling with God, the good news is that He also dwells in our hearts. The blueprint of life itself, Jesus with all the answers, chooses to dwell with us.

You can bring your giant questions to God. There are answers. There is a blueprint that points to salvation and eternal joy. It's a blueprint that's way better than any work of fiction turned into a splashy Tom Hanks movie. This story, this blueprint, is more true than anything in the universe. We'll look at the blueprint of the tabernacle in the coming days, but today we can be thankful that God has a plan and that He is sharing it with us.

The tabernacle was God's way of telling His people that there was hope. God had planned a way to dwell with His people and shared it first through the blueprint of the tabernacle, and then fully through Jesus Christ.

This hope is still true today. The answers are real. Jesus is real and He wants to tabernacle with us, today, right now, in your heart, and in mine.

DAY 20: LAMPSTAND

I'm a big fan of the Christmas tree. I am often the first person at the lot buying my tree the Saturday after Thanksgiving. And yes, I buy a live one. I like the smell of it and the swoosh of branches when I unclip the net and the tree explodes in the living room. We've had some disasters with trees over the years: giant gaping holes in the branches, falling trees, a bird nest, and many trees that had no intention of ever standing up straight.

Mostly what I like about the tree is the lights. We have a debate in our house about colored lights versus just white lights, but regardless of which way we go in any given year, I always want more. More lights! String 'em up!

I love the lights because, as anyone who lives in the northeast on the far eastern edge of the time zone knows and dreads, it's dark by 4:30 pm. For real. It's like we live in Alaska minus all the bears and salmon. I can hardly breathe when it's dark that early in the day, and the only way I can endure it is because the moment the sun sets, the Christmas tree lights go on.

People need light; I may need it more than most.

We are designed to need light. This is seen clearly in the tabernacle construction. In the outer room of the tabernacle, called the Holy Place, there were three main pieces of furniture, and one of them was the golden lampstand.

The tabernacle would have been dark without the lampstand; there were no windows. Practically speaking, the tabernacle needed to be illuminated in order for the priests to see what they were doing when they entered.

But it wasn't just a candelabra. God instructed Moses to build it in such a way that the lampstand looked like a tree. Actually, if you have Jewish friends, the lampstand looked like a bigger, more decorative version of the modern Menorah, which is also meant to remind people of a tree. Remember any interesting stories about trees in the Bible?

The first story, the story of creation, was a story about a tree--a tree that Adam and Eve should have been able to enjoy for all eternity. Instead, they decided to disobey God. Maybe they wanted more power or more control like the Israelites with their golden calf. However, by eating from the tree, instead of enriching their life, they lost it.

They were banished into the world, locked out of the garden by the cherubim who stand where God is enthroned in all His glory. Sin had a grip on their hearts, and they could no longer be in the presence of the Holy God. Sin and darkness became a part of the fabric of the human condition.

We feel that. Even if you live in a sunny, warm climate, there is a darkness inside us that is oppressive. It leads to hopelessness and despair, and ultimately it leads to being lost, because without light we cannot see.

Imagine the priests entering into the tabernacle, the one place on earth where they could encounter God, but without light they simply couldn't go further.

We're the same way. Without true light we can go no further. But Jesus says, "I am the light of the world. Anyone who follows me will never walk in darkness. They will have that light. They will have life." (John 8:12)

Never walk in darkness. Not at Christmas, not when your child is sick, not when you lose your job, not when your trust has been abused. Though there are shadows in this life, Jesus promises us we are never again going to walk in total darkness if we follow Him.

The golden lampstand stood to point the Israelites to their need for light and for life. Like all things in the tabernacle, it represented an ultimate reality.

Revelation 22 says that in heaven, in the new city and world where God dwells even now, there is a second tree of life that will bring healing, and "there will be no more night. They will not need the light of a lamp or the light of the sun. The Lord God will give them light." (Revelation 22:5)

This Christmas if your life is full of shadows, take hope. There is a day when there will be no darkness. As amazing as the golden lampstand was, there will be no need for it either. It represented the promise of true Light, and that Light came at Christmas and shines in our hearts today. It shines for you, and for me.

DAY 21: BREAD

Christmas lists. There, I said it. We could maybe have world peace if not for Christmas lists. Starting in the Fall, the Christmas ads begin. There are jingles and cutting edge special effects. There is big music; there is snow and mountains; there are puppies and babies and celebrities and dancing Santas, all urging us to make our Christmas list longer, more expensive and more perfect. So much energy and time and money and insanity... for what?

We open up the brand new kitchen mixer rocket ship insta spa aroma fitness device we were sure we wanted, but after one quick post on social media, the rocket ship gets thrown in a closet next to last year's rocket ship. Even worse, someone has to break down all the cardboard boxes. Is there anything more annoying than breaking down the cardboard after Christmas morning?

I know sometimes the Christmas list can be salvaged. Last Christmas my 14-year-old daughter and I surprised each other with the exact same pair of sneakers. We loved the sneakers, but even more we loved that we knew each other so well--and clearly both had great taste.

But moments like that are becoming rare. Christmas fatigue heightens the fact that the things we desire most can't generally be wrapped in a box. Perhaps what you really want is love from a family member, or a job that supports you. Maybe it's a marriage that needs restoration, or longing for a child, or for your own health. They aren't things that The Gap can weave into its annual striped sweater dance commercial. There is no car with a red bow on it that can actually bring us real joy.

God knows what we need. He knows what gives us real joy, and He began to show this to His people when He instructed Moses to build a table in the outer room, the Holy Place of the tabernacle where the bread of presence would sit. Each week the priests would eat it and replace it with new bread. Why? Was God hungry? Did the Divine Warrior God have some late night munchies? Of course not. The bread was never for God, it was always for His people.

While the Israelites were wandering in the wilderness, God famously provided manna for them each day. Bread from heaven. This was a God who would dwell with His people and also provide for His people. He gave them exactly what they needed, in the exact right timing.

Two thousand years later, Jesus would grow up to say, "I am the bread of life. Whoever comes to me will never go hungry, and whoever believes in me will never be thirsty." (John 6:35) Jesus, who was the bread of life in person, ate with His followers. In fact the Bible talks a lot about the meals Jesus ate. Jesus came in person to demonstrate His heart, the heart of God. God wants to be with us in all aspects of our lives, and He will dwell with us and provide for us.

Presence and provision. God's presence is in our lives, not in some theoretical way, but in the mundane trips to Home Depot, or in the line at the toll booth, or on the soccer field. God provides in the everyday moments of our lives. He gives us what we need, and He fulfills our deepest longing, a longing to live as we were created, as people designed in God's own image.

This Christmas I know we have our lists to make; but when you are shopping or, by now, as you wrap the cardboard boxes, you know the things you really long for. What is it that you feel you need in your heart? What is it that you desire in order to really feel like your life has value and meaning?

The answer should be the bread of life. The answer should be Jesus. He is what we most need at Christmas; and He is with us! God has always wanted to be with His people and has always provided what they need. He still does. He provides for you, and for me.

DAY 22: CLOTHING

Many years at our women's annual Christmas event at church we ask the attendees to wear a festive sweater--however they define it. Then we give out prizes for the best one--however we define it.

Frankly, I can't believe women own the stuff they own. They show up in all sorts of things. They wear the ugly Christmas sweaters, ornate hand appliquéd poinsettia sweaters, sweaters that light up, and some years we get head to toe outfits that look like Mrs. Claus fell into a knitting contest and came out bedazzled.

We have fun with it, but it does show that sometimes what you wear gives a glimpse into who you are. It's never a surprise when a certain lady shows up dressed like an elf and covered in flickering lights. She's just like that. She's outgoing and funny and doesn't take herself too seriously. It's also always reassuring to see another woman, one of our church matriarchs, show up in a lovely sweater covered in hand embroidered greenery. It's beautiful and tasteful and clearly meant for Christmas time. It highlights her beauty and grace and decades of service to our church.

Besides Christmas, and perhaps Easter if you count the itchy, scratchy dresses we make our daughters wear, we don't typically wear clothes themed for our faith or beliefs.

In constructing the tabernacle, though, God didn't just tell Moses what to build; He also told him what the priests should wear, because this was not just any job. The priest had the job of entering into the presence of the holy God once a year in the Holy of Holies, the room beyond the room where the lampstand and bread were.

Remember that the people couldn't even touch Mount Sinai when Moses received the instructions from God. Imagine being the priest who would work and serve within the tabernacle! It was such a formidable task that he had bells sewn into his tunic so that those outside could hear if he was still moving and walking--that is, that he was still alive.

Exodus 28 lists all the specific components that God required the priests to wear. Each component demonstrated some aspect of God's message to His people through the sacrificial system. One part, in particular, represented the tribes of Israel being brought into God's presence. It was the piece the priest wore across his chest. God said, "You shall make a breastpiece of judgment, in skilled work... There shall be twelve stones... like signets, each engraved with its name, for the twelve tribes." (ESV, Exodus 28:15-16, 21)

Whenever the priest entered into the Holy of Holies, into the presence of God, the twelve tribes were represented. Whenever the priest sought God's guidance in decisions to be made or, as the name implied, when judgments were to be made, the tribes were represented. Aaron was the first high priest, and God said, "Aaron shall bear the judgment of the people of Israel on his heart before the Lord regularly." (ESV, Exodus 28:30)

It's a little different than an ugly Christmas sweater. Wearing the judgment of your entire nation must have been a solemn and scary responsibility, because the judgment was always guilty. The whole tabernacle, the whole sacrificial system, was God's way of making His guilty people right with Him.

Guilt is an emotion we may feel more keenly at this time of year. Perhaps there are things you wish you had done differently; things you should have said, and now the year is over and it's too late. Maybe next year will be different, better. Maybe it won't.

But as the great hymn writer Charles Wesley wrote in 1742, "Arise, my soul, arise, shake off your guilty fears; the bleeding sacrifice, in my behalf appears."

Shake off your guilty fears! If not now--if not at Christmas--then when? We are not meant to wear judgment. We are not meant to carry guilt and shame. Our relationship to guilt changed when that little baby was born in Bethlehem. Jesus was born so that you do not need to feel guilty this Christmas. Jesus came so He could take our guilt and pay for it with His life, once and for all. This means "we have a great high priest who has passed through the heavens, Jesus, the Son of God... So let us boldly approach God's throne of grace. Then we will receive mercy. We will find grace to help us when we need it." (Hebrews 4:14,16)

Christ brings not only mercy and grace when we need it, but a new garment to wear. For we are not called to be the people outside the tabernacle waiting to hear the bells to make sure the priest is alive, but rather we ourselves are called to boldly approach the throne, wearing the garments that are described in Ephesians. We are to "put on the breastplate of righteousness." (ESV, Ephesians 6:14)

God's people no longer need a special priest wearing a garment representing judgment. Now His people are all invited to wear a new garment representing righteousness. Do you live as if you are still under judgment? Or have you shaken off your guilty fears? Do you live boldly as one who is free to approach the throne of God's grace?

This Christmas you can still wear your crazy sweaters. I say the uglier the better! But each day you should first make sure you are clothed in righteousness, celebrating the baby who makes your life free from guilt and shame. God wants to see His children clothed in righteousness, because He wants to see His children with Him. No more are we under judgment. Instead we have life. Free from guilt, free forever. It's true for you, and it's true for me.

DAY 23: ARK

One of my favorite modern Christmas songs is by singer-songwriter Andrew Peterson. It's titled *Matthew's Begats*. The lyrics are a musical version of Matthew 1, which is the genealogy of Jesus. I know that sounds weird. Trust me, it's a great song. I get it, genealogies are not often thought of as a particularly festive way to celebrate Christmas; but Jesus' genealogy is an exception that makes all the difference.

Matthew 1:1-16 traces His family line all the way back to Abraham. What you see is that His family tree includes a pretty rough set of characters. It wouldn't make for a great Christmas party introduction. "Hi, I'm Esther and in my family tree I have murderers, cheaters, incest and more! Want to be friends?" But that's what Jesus' lineage was like.

For example, this Messiah who came for God's chosen people of Israel had Gentiles in His line. Perhaps even more scandalous, in a time when family histories were not traced through women, Jesus had four women recorded in His line: two who were pagan, and one, Rahab, who was in a fairly unsavory line of business.

Matthew could have skipped over the women and just stuck to the names of their husbands. He could have glossed past some of the rough characters, like King Manasseh who threw his own son into a fire for a sacrifice. But Matthew listed the good, the bad and the ugly because the life and work of Jesus was for all of us--and we are rarely good, mostly bad, and often ugly.

While the Israelites were in the wilderness, it was clear that they, and not other people groups, were God's chosen people. They alone received the specific set of laws and practices so they could live with the one true God as their ruling King.

However, there were hints that this God and King had a plan that was much bigger. The biggest hint in the tabernacle, this blueprint that pointed to Jesus, was the Ark of the Covenant.

I know that as soon as you read that you, like me, thought of *Indiana Jones*. Let's pause. Take the moment you need to replay your favorite scene from the movie. Ok, now we can move on, though there's nothing I can do about the soundtrack being stuck in your head. Sorry.

The ark was a box covered in gold that held a variety of things including the tablets with the law written on them. More specifically, the ark was the only item placed in the Holy of Holies. The priest, wearing his bells, could only approach the ark once a year on the Day of Atonement. You probably have heard it called by its Hebrew name, Yom Kippur.

The ark had two things on top of it. First, it had a lid that God called the "mercy seat" which is tied to the Hebrew word for atonement. Once a year the priest would sprinkle blood on the ark's cover and "atone" for the sins of the nation of Israel.

On top of the lid were two cherubim made of gold. They guarded the cover because above the cover was where God allowed His presence to manifest in the cloud or fire. As we saw from the burning bush, or Mount Sinai, when God was present He showed it in some recognizable form such as fire, wind or clouds. People could not approach without specific invitation and instructions from God.

So how does this Ark of the Covenant relate to Matthew 1? Matthew looked back to a lot of people in Jesus' genealogy who, at a glance, had no hope of entering into the Holy of Holies or drawing near to the mercy seat of God to atone for their actions. People a lot like us. Then Matthew looked at Jesus. Maybe you think this whole Jesus-came-at-Christmas thing is all well and good for most people, but you have a pretty big secret in your life. If people really knew you, or knew what you've thought or done, they'd be horrified.

Good. You're just the sort of person who can sign up for Christmas.

Jesus was born at Christmas so that He Himself could approach the mercy seat and atone for all of us. One final Day of Atonement and then no more. There is no corner, no spot in your life, or heart too dark, too far gone, too remote that it can't be reached by Jesus. In fact, He's already atoned for the darkest of dark corners.

Hebrews 2:17 says, "So He [Jesus] had to be made like people, fully human in every way. Then he could serve God as a kind and faithful high priest. And then he could pay for the sins of the people by dying for them."

Behind the phrase "pay for the sins" in that verse is a fancy Greek word for atonement--a word loved by theologians. In English the word is sometimes translated as "propitiation." (There isn't a test at the end, don't worry.) Specifically, the word means the covering of our sins, the atoning for sins in every corner of our heart--every single part of it.

Jesus did that for us. He covered our sins like the mercy seat covered the ark. He spilled His blood to atone for us, as the priests spilled the blood of the animals. However, when Jesus did this for us it did not need to be done again. It was enough to atone for all the murderers, the schemers, the gossipers, the angry, the bitter, and the deceptive people-- that is, to atone for us.

Now, whoever we are, whatever our background, we are welcome to approach God Himself. The cherubim will not hold us back. God will be present in our lives and in our hearts. God looks at us and does not see the dark corners; He only sees the perfect life and work of Jesus. It doesn't matter who you are, what your history is, who you're related to, or what you secretly did last week.

What matters is that Jesus invites you into the Holy of Holies, not once a year but every day. The Holy of Holies is where God dwells, and if we follow Him, He chooses to dwell in our hearts. He invites all of us, no matter our lineage or life. He wants you to enter into His presence, into His family tree. He calls us to approach Him, always and forever. He calls you, and He calls me.

DAY 24: GLORY

One of the things that stresses me out the most about event planning, whether for church or just in my own life, is a fear that no one will show up. I think it's rooted in an episode early in our marriage when my husband and I were visiting churches in Memphis where we lived for two years. One Sunday after visiting a church that was quirky but friendly, the pastor grabbed our hands on our way out and said, "I want to come over and get to know you! Let's pick a date right now." And so we did. We picked an evening that week to invite him over to our first apartment--all 700 square feet of it.

We didn't even own three chairs, but we cleaned our small space, brewed coffee, and I made lemon bars (out of a box mix, as I certainly didn't know how to cook; ok, let's be honest, I'd still use a box mix).

We both had office jobs, but after work, rather than changing into comfy clothes we kept on our nice work outfits and we waited. And waited. And... he was a no-show. It meant more lemon bars for us, and we eventually found a church we enjoyed, but it felt weird and sad when it happened.

Thankfully, the women who work on our events team are astute enough to guesstimate attendance numbers based on reality, instead of my neurosis, and I trust them to sort out how much food to buy and how many name tags to make up.

But imagine if you were the Israelites.

God commanded you to build this elaborate tabernacle, detailing every single bit of it--all the furniture, the coverings, the layout, the priestly garments. He gave them a full-blown plan designed to make a way for Him to dwell among His people; a full system so they could atone for their sins and live with God as their King.

But in the end would it matter? Would God actually show up? The people had seen the pillar of fire and smoke on the mountain and in their wanderings, but would God really come and dwell in a tabernacle that was situated right in the middle of their dusty camp of smelly people?

What would happen? God was always the main character in Exodus, but in the end, did He really want to come dwell among these people? Does He actually want to dwell with you?

Here it is: tomorrow is Christmas. Can God really work a miracle in your heart and in your life? Can you be sure He will show up--that He wants to be with you?

Oh, but my friends, He does show up!

In the last four verses of the last chapter of Exodus we see the final scene: "Then the cloud covered the tent of meeting. The glory of the Lord filled the holy tent. Moses couldn't enter the tent of meeting because the cloud had settled on it. The glory of the Lord filled the holy tent." (Exodus 40:34-35)

God's glory was so brilliant, so awesome, that even Moses who had spent 40 days on Mount Sinai with God couldn't go near it. God showed up, He was there, and He stayed there and led His people onward towards the promised land.

Yes, there was an entire system in place to keep the unholy people out of the glory presence of the one Holy God, but all they had to do was look towards the tabernacle and by day they'd see the cloud and by night they'd see the fire, and they'd know that this God was real and He wanted to dwell among them.

This Christmas it's still true. God shows up. He came as a baby so that He could dwell with us first as a man on earth, and now in Spirit in our very hearts. Every day. Every minute. Every second. No matter how dark the road is, how hard the season can be, how deeply you may think you've failed or how alone and scared you may be, He's here.

God shows up to dwell with you. Jesus comes as Immanuel, "God with us." That's what tomorrow is all about. Even better, you do not have to wait until tomorrow for this to be true; you don't have to doubt it if you thought maybe this wasn't actually for you. Jesus says, "And you can be sure that I am always with you, to the very end." (Matthew 28:20)

To the very end, from the very beginning. Because in the beginning, at creation itself, God showed up.

He will never fail you, He will never leave you, He will never let you down. Jesus no longer has to come in smoke and fire, but He still comes with all the power of the God of the universe--to you. He comes directly to you.

This Christmas we can trust that God shows up. Don't live your life wondering if He will. Tomorrow we celebrate that He always does. He always shows up for you, and He always shows up for me.

Esther C. Baird

DAY 25: CHRISTMAS

It's Christmas!!!! If you have children you are either reading this at 2 am (the only hour you will find quiet on this day) or you've already torn through the gifts, made and cleaned up three meals, and are pretty sure you accidentally re-gifted a set of scented candles, but no one, yet, has noticed.

Regardless of your situation, whether it's hectic or quiet, stressful or lonely, warm and sunny, or snowy and cold, nothing in the whole world can change the fact that it is December 25th.

Some things don't change, like the date of Christmas. So I'm going to keep this short, because I know we have things to do and places to go and naps to take. Plus we finished Exodus. God showed up and the rest, as they say, is history.

History that is only beginning to be written...

Exodus is only the second book of the Bible. You should see how God showed up in Judges or Ruth. You can't believe the things God did when He showed up in Zechariah or Isaiah.

Then of course there's the whole New Testament where He actually walked and talked on earth as a man. Or later when He showed up as the Spirit empowering the men and women who traveled and taught the promises of God through the lands of the early church; the promises that spread throughout the world and across time, all the way to now, to us, to this Christmas day.

Today we can celebrate that God shows up every day in the hearts and lives of those who follow Him.

This Christmas it is my prayer that by looking at Exodus you saw how much God loves us and wants to be with us. How He planned to show up since before the beginning of time. How He foreshadowed Jesus through the life of Moses. How He used the plagues, Passover, and escape from Egypt to teach us about our lives and our need for rescue and a new land. How His original Christmas card, the Ten Commandments, are not old and irrelevant, but alive and full of God's words to us about life with Him. And how that blueprint for the tabernacle was not just a middle-school diorama project, but was the very life and work of Jesus explained through a building so that the Israelites could begin to anticipate the amazing things God was promising.

God's been showing up across all time, because He wants to dwell with us, with you. On Christmas we celebrate that He made that possible through Jesus.

Christmas does not need to fill you with dread or stress. Yes, our world is busy. Yes, this time of year is harder in many ways. But if we are children of God's promises than true peace is ours because we follow the Prince of Peace who was born that Christmas morning, who the prophet Isaiah named a thousand years before He was born:

> For to us a child is born,
> to us a son is given,
> and the government will be on his shoulders.
> And he will be called
> Wonderful Counselor, Mighty God,
> Everlasting Father, Prince of Peace. (NIV, Isaiah 9:6)

The Prince of Peace came. He showed up. It's all real and it always has been. Exodus is an amazing book in the giant story of God's plan for all of us. God's Christmas plan is real, and it's always been real for you, and for me.

Esther C. Baird

ACKNOWLEDGMENTS

This all started when I casually suggested to my lead pastor, Greg Hills, that Exodus might make a good Christmas sermon series, further, I'd like to do the supporting research. Next thing I knew I had a book outline in place. So, thank you to my pastors for agreeing to my ideas (most of the time)! Thank you to the globetrotting preacher, Ray Pritchard, for answering ALL of my questions and for so enthusiastically supporting me along the way. My Dad, George Lawrence, taught me how to write when I was a little girl and has been my behind-the-scenes editor ever since. He edited this first draft—no easy task with a daughter prone to longwinded riffs. Thanks, Dad! The hip and lovely Bryn Limmer was my technical editor, she found inconsistencies and typos till she probably slipped into a coma, but I think we're still friends! Of course none of this could happen without my husband, Les, who supported me when I announced, "Hey, I think I'm going to write a devotional this summer." He loves me even when I get obsessed, and I love him for it. Lastly, thanks to my favorite two daughters, Abby and Riley. You ate a lot of terrible dinners during this process. I'd like to say things will be better now, but I think we all know that's unlikely. Still, I love you; so that should count for something.

-Esther Baird, October 18, 2018.

Esther C. Baird